Standen

Embrace y

Love HDavis.

Embrace

Your

WOW Factor

7 Steps to Love Yourself Free of Apologies and Free of Excuses

Paris Love

Copyright Page

Ordering information
Special discounts are available for quantity purchases. Includes biographical references and index.

Table of Contents

DEDICATION

I dedicate this book to Skyler Milan Smith and Ellasia Ashton Payne. You are the WOW Factor.

Foreword

By Serita Jakes

The Potter's House
Dallas, Texas

There are many acronyms for **WOW**, including Women of Worship, Women of Worth, and many more.

But in the pages of this missive penned from the heart of Paris Love, every woman who hides behind the mask of low self-esteem and brokenness will find their path to being freed from the chains that bind.

This book is a survival manual for those who've faced the raging flames of life, but trust that they will come out as pure gold! Elevate your mind, shed your inhibitions, embrace the NOW, and be transformed from the inside out!

You are better than the hateful whispers that have infringed upon your rest and the trespassing glances that haunt you. You will be empowered to step out of your despair. You will be challenged to exchange your mourning for gladness. You will find a garment of praise instead of the rags that you've worn much too long.

WOW? Might I suggest that you define it as, "Wounded Over Words," that we cannot un-hear? Or maybe to some of us it maybe defined that we are, "Weary Of Worry?"

But, Paris Love would not leave us wrapped in disparity. She unravels the mystery that will unction us to "Walk On Water" because someone greater than you and I has summoned us to break free from regret and take control of our lives and finally "Witness Overwhelming Wonder" that is designated just for YOU!

WOW! You say?

Indeed so!

ADVANCED PRAISE

Paris Love has written an honest and thought-provoking book. She strips down the facade that most women tend to put on and asks us to truly embrace our inner beauty and strength.

The **WOW Factor** isn't about the physical but the spiritual energy that we all possess and bring to the world. She wants us all to lead with that positive energy and watch our dreams become more than just wishes, but become reality! **WOW!**
Vee Critton

Having observed her maturation from adolescence into a successful mother, budding artist, fashion stylist/strategist, author, and entrepreneur, Paris has routinely shown her ability to enlighten, inspire, and encourage the best in all of us.

In her latest effort through the printed word, she very ably describes the journey of self-discovery women must take in developing and strengthening their sense of self-worth. Replete with examples of her own life, Paris commands us to power through our own self-examination inside and out. She then motivates us to embrace our true selves and to branch out and share it with loved ones and the world.

Paris touts the value of a balanced life. We should be at peace with what we can accomplish for others but also foster continuous self-improvement and development.

Embrace Your WOW Factor is a true testament to a life lived through constant evaluation, encouragement, and a fierce desire to be the best self one can be. This book is a must read!

Dr. Barbara P. Jackson, President
JFA and Associates
Las Vegas, NV

After reading and reviewing Paris Love's new book, I concluded that it was an extraordinarily candid conversation with herself that she eloquently conveyed to the reader on how to personally stay woke in times of balancing family life and your career!

I was moved by Paris' ability and willingness to allow time for healing and realizing that growth is not an overnight work! Overall, I believe this young sister has tapped into a power greater than prosperity, pain, and even the process—it's called Life and Love.

It appears to me that millions of readers here and abroad will be able to glean from the simplicity of surrendering it all to God and allowing the Holy Spirit to take charge!

What a delicious dialogue she shared with us about blessings, balance, and the intentional efforts it requires to be better.

Sensational!

Pastor John Currie

Grateful Fellowship Community Church

Desoto, Texas

Acknowledgements

Peace and Blessings!

My dearest thanks to the Most High God for blessing me to Embrace My WOW Factor.

Thanks to my family and friends for adjusting to my moods over the past years and to my wonderful clients who have shared their lives and stories to aid me in creating this journey that ultimately led to this book.

With Love,
Paris Love

Servicing celebrity clients is a routine part of what I do. One client in particular always stood out to me, however, discretion demands I keep her name silent. She exemplified the word beautiful in every sense of it's meaning. She was tall, toned, talented, and able to turn the heads of both men and women. She walked into the salon with an air of success and superiority yet she was plagued by pain. It was obvious to me that she was seeking an inner peace.

She was not nice although she could have been. There was no apparent reason for her to be as rude and unkind as she was. This demeanor was the antithesis of the beauty she possessed. An ugly attitude can erase all traces of physical beauty. I reacted as did everyone that came across her with mild dismay—until I realized she was really in pain.

I was able to sense her hurt as she tried to lash out and hurt others. It was then that I came to uncover the same need in myself for a better way to express the painful issues of my life. I realized I was mirroring her pain. It was then that the WOW Factor was downloaded in my spirit. I accepted the fact that I had to learn to control my emotions and expressions. At that point, judgment was irrelevant, and I surrendered my ego and began the journey of EMBRACING my WOW Factor!

Into to the WOW

I am Paris Love (formerly Paris Payne) and I'm a style influencer. I've spent many years in the beauty industry as a hairstylist and style consultant working with some of the most celebrated people on the planet. I've been in the presence of women who are gorgeous just waking up in the morning. As a stylist and consultant, I've gone into the homes of powerful professionals, celebrities, and stars to help them organize and orchestrate a look that compliments them.

Over the course of many years, I began to see a trend that has developed among women that are on a quest for beauty. The trend is that once the outside had been transformed, the inside was still unadorned. Every person is a canvas waiting to be painted and transformed into a work of art. They are a lump of clay waiting to be fashioned by a sculptor to become beautiful, magnificent, and incredible women, worthy of **WOW**. But, they have to know where to find it.

I had found that once these incredible creatures have been transformed into everything they could imagine on the outside that looks and appears beyond beautiful, many women still have a self-image that is skewed. Some see an image that they think is not perfect or complete. What I found in my experiences was that, "Perfection is not possible, but excellence is." Excellence is a part of that **WOW** Factor that says, "I'm willing and able to do everything I can to enhance the package, and that's enough."

I discovered that the interior is more important than the exterior. When a woman or person works on making sure that the interior is beautiful and worthy of respect, admiration, and desire, the outside automatically conforms, reforms, and transforms. Too many celebrities, professional women, and women from all walks of life have been transformed on the outside and appear to be beautiful. Yet, once you meet their attitude and experience their inner expression, you would be shocked at their fractured inner image. Often the public face that appears to be happy and excited about life, is struggling to maintain that persona. What you see is only a mask for an interior that is full of pain, regret, and self-loathing. How can a woman that has been transformed so beautifully on the outside to look like the epitome of everything is in essence slipping away into the darkness of her interior?

What's missing? This is the question that I asked after years and years of transforming ordinary women into extraordinary creatures. These women were beautiful on the outside but they still believed they needed refinement and other artificial expressions to conform to worldly standards. I observed more and more broken women, polished on the outside, yet cracked and crumbling on the inside. I saw a double standard being used against themselves, by themselves. I saw feelings of unworthiness, non-acceptance, and low self-esteem.

How can someone so beautiful be so empty on the inside? That was the question that I often asked myself as I saw the result of my work. I've been responsible for every aspect of outer beauty from hair, make-up, and wardrobe to completely transforming women into a world standard of glamour. All too many of them are walking in pain and brokenness. The pain of not being enough, the brokenness of trying to be better, and yet not measuring up—even in their own minds.

EMBRACE Your **WOW** Factor was born out of these heartbreaking observations and revelations. God began to speak and show me that it is possible to be beautiful, but that beauty begins on the inside. If you haven't accepted the possibility and the poignancy of your own beauty, no amount of exterior transformation can cause that change to occur. It begins in the mind, heart, and then extends to the surface.

I've traveled throughout the country speaking to women and many of them express these feelings of not being worthy enough. The principles that I present in this book, EMBRACE Your WOW Factor, 7 Ways to Love Yourself, Free of Apologies and Excuses, are extremely significant and necessary for women who want to begin to accept and love themselves and become capable of accepting and loving others. Take time to explore the principles because they have been downloaded from The Divine. This divine download speaks directly to the issues facing each of us that are born out of experiences in our lives. Some of these experiences have told us that we're not worthy and have convinced us that we are not acceptable.

Once you EMBRACE Your **WOW**, (Which is the Spirit of God that lives within you), you will realize that nothing on the exterior is comparable to the beauty, the elegance, the style, and the significance that exists on the inside. When you know who you are and you love who you are, then you're able to embrace your **WOW**. I invite you to take this journey with me as I share with you how to **EMBRACE Your WOW Factor.**

*The **WOW Factor** is synonymous for the **Holy Spirit.** It's my spirit, my confidence, and my assurance. It's me knowing with unwavering faith that I am here and I am awesome. This God-given confidence is our gift and birthright from God!*

Paris

Section I

Welcome to Your WOW!

The world is full of awesome and amazing people, places, and things. ***On my journey to discovering and accepting myself, I learned that I'm pretty amazing and awesome.*** We all are. Yet we allow ourselves to be bamboozled by the negative things that happen to us. All too often we are betrayed by the ones we love, and more often than not, we betray ourselves.

I woke up one day abandoned by the one whom I pledged my love, affection, and devotion. I did not see it coming. For too long, I blamed myself and cocooned myself in a shell of frustration and fear. I feared I would never love or live again. I had poured myself into my relationship and did not see the clear signs that it was troubled. When I woke from my nightmare, I realized I had two amazing people depending on me to help shape them into the awesome women they were destined to become. I finally realized that there is love after love—and I deserved to live it.

That is when I discovered and began to **Embrace my WOW Factor**. I had to believe I was indeed a Woman of

Worth. I needed to accept that I was worthy of winning. Once I realized my own true self, I was able to reinvent myself.

Today, I am a successful entrepreneur, a great mom, speaker, author, artist, and **WOW** Life Strategist. This is my story of how I regained myself and discovered the new me. The question that you should be asking by now is, "How did I get it?"

Each of us possesses two natures inside of us. One is the WOE Focus, who shouts, "Woe is me!" and asks the questions, "Why am I going through this?" "Why is this happening to me?" or "Why me?" This is a defeatist attitude. This is the reason most people get stuck. I have found when you focus on failure, you invite more failure and lack into your life. You get more of what you focus on. Those people who engage in their WOE focus are in essence saying, "Woe" to their future.

On the other hand, there's the **WOW** Factor. This is where self-love and self-appreciation live and rule. Those people who embrace their **WOW** Factor look at life as a blessing and an incredible opportunity to overcome and win. They see failure as a chance to learn and grow.

When we realize our **WOW Factor**, we see only sunshine, even when it rains. That is not to say there are no seasons of lack or attack. It just means we approach those times as a part of a process and not the end of our progress. The **WOW Factor** is a way to look at life and deal with it from a position of gratitude and joy. It draws on the positive possibility versus the negative appearance.

We can all choose to live in the **WOW**. These are the women who can smile at their trials and find joy in their journey, even if it has a few bumps and bruises. I have decided to embrace my **WOW** and show others how to discover and embrace theirs as well.

Now we come to me, and how I went from WOE to **WOW**. My backstory starts with my marriage, my children, and being blinded by love on the day I found out that there were problems in my relationship. I looked up and asked, "What's the matter with me? How can I survive? How could I be so naïve? It must have been my fault. What am I going to do now? What about the kids? How could you?" This was the day I discovered my **WOW**.

Through pain and agony every day and living the realization that something was terribly wrong. Waiting for relief and not seeing it coming was depressing. Then **WOW**! I started praying and believing God for a change. When I didn't see the change coming, I stopped asking for aid in my marriage, and started transforming myself.

I just started feeling better day by day in the Word, experiencing higher vibrations in the morning, seeking God, and being grateful for the beautiful things, which were always there. Nature, the laughter of the children, doing something that I enjoyed as an art form, and being around people were all yummy pleasures that were returning to me. Life was a gift worth living, and I accepted the invitation.

When I started being grateful, that's when I saw the shift in my life happen. I was waking up every day the same person in the same place of misery. As I began to transform and share my story with other people, they went from being encouraging to making it obvious that I was getting on their nerves. People will listen to you to a certain degree, and then they get aggravated. They lose the empathy for you and then they just want a new story from you. That's when I felt that nudge of, "Nobody wants to hear this anymore," and I realized that all I have is God and myself, and that is enough.

That took me in another direction and caused me to focus on the inside. Once I went inside, there was no coming out. By then, my husband had moved upstairs. I thought that was the worst thing that could happen. The detachment and disconnection were heart wrenching. The absence of him was not something that made my heart grow fonder. Too be honest, I ached and wanted things to be as they were. The truth is they would never be the same and I needed to accept that truth.

That time alone with God gave me the room for reflection and growth. It was a little lonely. Yet the most unexpected thing happened—I began to discover me.

In the solitude is where the magic happens. This is where I meditate and journal. This is where I pray and praise. Here is where my healing began. I found that everything became lighter. Nothing is as awful as it seems. This was truly the first of an endless stream of **WOW**! These moments changed my life and challenged me to become better and not bitter. These moments taught me to appreciate all the beauty and awesomeness that the world offered that I had been missing and taking for granted.

I prepared myself for his departure. The fear of him leaving was no longer a threat. I now encouraged it. I found excitement in imagining myself alone. I needed some 'me time' to develop my **WOW**. I began to believe ***Not only do I have me, I enjoy me.***

I started eating alone and enjoying the solitude. I started doing more things by myself. I contemplated my next steps through this journey and got excited about my freedom. In doing so, God started sowing seeds, dropping knowledge of love, gratitude, excitement, and anticipation. I didn't know what exactly was coming, but I knew it would be good. I applied my faith in God the whole time.

WOW Fact: It's OK to be by yourself. Time alone is time with God and it allows you to reflect and redirect your energy so that you learn how to love yourself!

Each day, I began to say to myself, "Hello, I'm here! I'm great! I'm wonderful, and everything I'm lacking in the marriage I found within myself. It's more than enough. Actually, it's much more than enough! This is the basis of how I got out of that place and to the place I am now."

This place of accomplishment and assurance is the place of **WOW**! I thought at one point what happened in the relationship was my fault. However, my alone time allowed me to stop internalizing whose fault it was. Instead, my own self-analysis urged me to forgive him, forgive myself, and begin to live my life FREE of apologies and excuses.

One of my favorite scriptures is Psalms 91:1-2, which reads, "Whoever dwells in the shelter of the Most High will rest in the shadow of the Almighty. I will say of the Lord, 'He is my refuge and my fortress, My God, in whom I trust.'"

The Word focuses on trusting God and I lived in that place! That is where I resided and that's where I found my refuge. In doing so, I studied my inner connectivity. You must apply anything that's positive to your life. You can't keep reading books, gathering affirmations, and getting these powerful nuggets and not apply them. These are messages from God.

All of this is a part of the journey because they're in your midst for a reason. At this point I decided to let go of the pain of the past and accept my new world of joy and inner peace.

In the scriptures and most of the motivational books I read, they were all in alignment with the phrase, **"Be free of Apologies. Be free of Excuses."** In retrospect whatever happened that got me in this place was a blessing. It was time to be free of blaming and take full responsibility.

I took responsibility for my part in the demise of my relationship. In the realm of things, it was not just the separation and the divorce, but the lack of communication and the absence of me in the relationship, within myself, and in my relationship with God.

I hadn't been giving God His time. Therefore, I felt He hadn't been listening to my prayers during a time where I was so desperate to be heard by God and by others. People don't always have time, but God always has time when you make time for Him.

When I stopped being the victim and started taking responsibility for my part, it was easy for me to forgive. **You must forgive.** The hardest thing was forgiving myself and saying, **"Listen, he was in your life for a purpose and a reason."**

I started listing the blessings that came out of the relationship. It was not just the marriage. We were buddies for years prior to getting married and we had a great time. We had a child together.

I highlighted what was good in him and what attracted me to him in the first place. There were things such as his kindness and giving personality. He was an excellent father and provider. For most people, those characteristics would be enough. At the time it was enough for me. Yet there were other issues that kept us at odds.

Again, I took responsibility and I forgave him. It was a process. After forgiving him, people couldn't believe how happy I was. I transformed overnight. Even my ex-husband couldn't understand how I was so open and receptive to him. Our arguments became fewer and less intense. I stopped questioning him regarding his whereabouts and focused more on my serenity. He was perplexed as to how I could be calm in the storm we both weathered.

At first, the changes were subtle. Yet I can remember the day I prioritized my happiness as opposed to my love for the relationship. My desire to love myself was greater than loving anyone else. My power wasn't taken—I gave it away willingly. Instead of destroying me, it empowered me. He was astonished at my newfound confidence, and realized that the threat of losing him was over.

It is easy to forgive knowing that God has forgiven me. I released the stress and anger, embraced fearlessness, and stepped into knowing and believing in myself. With these series of steps, you get so high that you can touch the sky. The present moment will be all that matters. You can reside in this place with bliss.

It's so incredible. Forgiveness erased the bitterness. I was able to like myself. That made life much more fulfilling and enjoyable. By letting go, I was able to grow.

First, I had to identify the pain, look at it for what it was, and then take responsibility for my part. I was free of blaming myself and beating myself up. I got out of God's way and allowed Him to do the work in me. That meant that I was using the following two principles:

1. Trusting the process of prayer and
2. Reading the scriptures and applying the word.

It also meant that I was truly relaxing and allowing God's sovereignty to express itself.

We often have a tendency to step in and DO SOMETHING, when God is saying, "I Got This!" In time the pain subsided, and the harshness fell away. I was able to get up and not just focus on the reality of my situation, but also the wholeness of my life.

I moved from a place of anger and frustration to a place of sheer gratitude for everything. Now I wake up and realize I have life, food, clothes, shelter, and I start thanking God for everything. I allow God to be a part of everything.

My turning point was when I began speaking life as I desired, despite my current reality. The depressed me had to go. She was replaced with a woman that was created from the pain of her past and the transformation had begun. That's when I started affirming a wonderful woman of God, a woman of intrigue, and a consciousness that was divine.

The change was evident to others. People started telling me, **"WOW! Something is different about you!"** I knew what it was.

Now I'm unstoppable! Just like you created a place of sadness and depression for yourself, when you shift to a place of bliss and excitement for your life, it just gets better. I stayed focused going forward. I know with unwavering faith that everything that happened to me, the time it happened, and the way it happened was pre-ordained to grow me into this amazing place of, **WOW!**

I used to say I'd do it all over again. But why should I? It's been done. I've conquered my fears. What's the worst thing that could happen? If he leaves or if my job happens to change, everything that I feared, I conquered. **The good thing is that there's Love after Love. WOW!**

There was a book waiting to be birthed from my experience. I can motivate and inspire others. I have a story to tell, and it must be told. It's my life's purpose to do so before I leave this earth. I can go on and on with all the good things that came out of this experience. Things had to happen, and I know that now. God will get your attention, and until you get the memo, and acknowledge it, He will keep sending them to you.

When you finally get the message, apply it, and say, **"OK, this is what God sent for me. This is today's assignment.**

This is what I'm supposed to ingest. This is what I am supposed to apply."

Now the work for your life is fulfilling. Yes, it's for you to get and also to share. You can't keep this kind of stuff inside or keep it to yourself. It's not a secret anymore. It's for other people who also desire to get relief. I know this is my mission to aid in someone else's healing and journey.

I have allowed the pain of my past to paint a picture for others to see that they can stay stuck in their pain or move forward toward a better place. If you go forward, you grow, and what's in front of you is, **WOW**!

I went from a point of pain to a point of passion and purpose by reinventing myself and removing the scales of the past. This is how I learned how to like, love, and enjoy myself.

I Had to Slow Down

Everything was going really fast the first few years. My career was moving, prospering, and growing. I was living in the home of my dreams and driving my dream car. I had more money in the bank than I could ever imagine. Life was good and getting better with each day. Consequently, I missed a lot of time with my children by focusing on my career.

Once we accomplished all these things and settled into our respective areas, we thrust ourselves into it. I became consumed with the money and the limelight. I was so busy, and I did so well that I didn't even take time to breathe, enjoy, or savor my accomplishments.

I didn't take time out to see my children grow up. I missed their sports events and those tender moments that only a mom should have been privy to. Those moments are irreplaceable and the children quite often reminded me of how they suffered due to my absence. Now I can't recollect because I was so busy building my empires that

I missed a very important part of the equation—the children. Parenting was replaced with payments and payouts. I thought if they had the material things that would be plenty.

Once you create a method that works for you and your family, then you can embrace life easier. It's more than possible. Now I get up with a purpose, and I take time out with God and with myself. Life is more organized now and detailed. I now prioritize what's important for me and my journey. That purpose is to stay in the now. Enjoy each moment. What's going to happen next year or next week is irrelevant. My focus is embracing life and savoring every aspect of it, including the children, my career, and most of all me!

My journey went from pain to becoming a **WOW** Woman. I put the oxygen mask on me first, as opposed to trying to save everyone else. I was then able to save myself, and in saving myself first, I can now offer a rescue plan for others.

As women, we are helpmates and mothers and often lose ourselves in the process. Yet there still must be a balance. Even though we focus on our careers and the family, what about focusing on you as a woman? If you put the family and career before the woman, you lose yourself to them along the way, and then you become frustrated and tired.

The very things that you ask God for, including education, career, and marriage, can become a lot of work! It can become tiresome and mundane. It can weigh you down. You may even have feelings of regret.

God's blessings shouldn't weigh you down. They should elevate and motivate you to inspire others. Those things are beautiful within themselves. All of these things are blessings you must prioritize. If you consume yourself with preparing dinner, structuring the family, the children's events, and day-to-day tasks of life, then you didn't take time out for yourself.

You have to be careful not to allow your family to become too depend on you. It will be very easy to lose yourself in the process. For me, I know that I must prioritize. God first, then me, and then family. If I consume myself with keeping them afloat, then I sink.

When You Start Complaining, You Can't Praise

For instance, you get with your girlfriends at cocktail hour and say how difficult it is at home because you can't seem to get time for yourself. It's neither up to your husband nor the children. It's up to you. You have to demand time for yourself and take it.

Be the solution! Build yourself. Grow yourself to the point that you're so full and you're so good for the family, you're able to enhance and guide them sufficiently. You're able to give back to the family. If you're empty at that point, then you can't pour into them.

The **WOW Factor** is synonymous for the **Holy Spirit.** It's my spirit, my confidence, and my assurance. It's me knowing with unwavering faith that I am here, and I am better. Not only am I better, I am great, and I am grateful.

The **WOW** is how you feel. It's a movement and a state of mind. Now, it's up to you to tap into it. We all possess the **WOW**. It's a rebirth, a calling, an awakening of such mass proportions that you float, you glide, and you're seamless.

When negative things come your way, you have a shifting mechanism that you didn't even know you had. You have now become powerful. All these things are of God and you connecting with God. Therefore, the God in you, The Holy Spirit, gives the power to live in the **WOW**.

You were born this way. You simply forgot your power. You simply put your power and energy into negative things, and now that you're getting back to the root of your existence, it's easy, it's exciting, and you look forward to every day because you know you're winning. You know you're winning because you're alive and you're better for it. Anything in the past is over. Your future can't reflect on your past, and your NOW is exciting, rewarding, and fulfilling.

The phrase **I remember when** takes on a whole new perspective. **I remember when** becomes your ally, not your enemy. **I remember when** becomes your best friend because now the place you're in, at this present moment, is all that matters. Now that place is a place of elation and celebration!

Now when I can say, "**I remember when,**" and I get goose bumps because I know I'm winning. I believe it, and now I'm sharing that belief through this book, **EMBRACE Your WOW Factor: 7 Steps To Love Yourself, Free of Apologies and Excuses.** I share the principles I used to achieve that belief.

Too many people have gotten stuck from stuff in their past breakups, losses, disappointments, and frustrations. They don't look forward to the next day. They wake up hurting in pain, and some even wake up wanting to end their lives. If you EMBRACE Your **WOW** Factor, you can wake up every day excited!

WOW Facts:
- *When you find the strength to forgive yourself and others, you become a better person.*
- *Look forward to each day and you will discover something to look forward to in each day.*
- *When you start complaining, you stop praising.*
- *Be free of blame.*
- *Be free of apologies and excuses.*

<u>The Inevitable</u>

Section II

Let's talk about seven ways that you can **EMBRACE** Your **WOW** and change your NOW to something that you are excited about. We're going to use the word **EMBRACE** to plan a roadmap for winning.

Go Within

<u>Enjoy Everyday Life</u>
It's Time to Apply the SWITCH MODE!

Chapter 1

E: Enjoy Everyday Life

Let's start with, **E**, the first letter in **EMBRACE**. The question for this section is, "How can you **Enjoy Everyday Life** with expectancy?" The wonderful thing about going to bed with excitement is that you wake up with expectancy. Therefore, **Enjoying Everyday Life** starts with a visualization exercise the night before. As you fall asleep, you visualize the next day in the **WOW**. It has to marinate in your spirit throughout the night. After prayer, you fall asleep free of worries. You look forward to the next morning with anticipation.

You must wake up with good vibrations and claiming a **WOW** filled day. You visualize styling yourself and getting dressed for the day. You're now at work in your visualization where you're friendly, kind, and getting

Power Points done. You're growing and you're aiding others.

Next, you're home cooking dinner and you're in your best place. You're helping the children with their homework. These things happen in your visualization. Many people wake up and go about their day with no hope of it being their best day possible. When you **EMBRACE Your WOW,** you go to bed focused on a **WOW** filled day and wake up feeling what you visualized the night before. That process keeps you rooted and grounded in your **WOW**.

When you get up in the morning, spend some time with yourself. Set aside at least 15–20 minutes prior to getting dressed and starting your day. Spend some time in solitude. That's your time with God and that's the time that you're developing in quietness.

This allows you to go from that place of difficulty and frustration to one of rhythm, passion, and drive that is exciting and joyful. From that place, the rest of the day gets easier.

So, how does a woman that is stuck, get to the point where she begins to enjoy one day, much less every day? It starts with one day at a time. I alluded to it by saying that you go to bed at night with excitement, and then you wake up with that expectancy because you are visualizing what the day is going to bring.

What if you hit a bump in the course of the day? What if things are going great and your vision is becoming clear, then something happens to make it cloudy or cause you some frustration? What do you do and how do you keep enjoying the day despite distractions that could arise?

That is a question that often comes up. This is where you utilize **The Switch Mode**. You must know that things are going to happen. I affirm who I am while I'm brushing my teeth. I take a moment. I feel what that feels like. Then I go into **The Switch Mode.**

You must switch your perspective sometimes. It could take days, sometimes weeks, or it could take minutes to switch, depending on what the news is. Life happens, but what's important to know in making **The Switch** is not how long it takes. It doesn't matter what it is, **just do it.** You must switch or you will stay in the mindset of negativity.

The Switch Mode is an aid to get you back to that place of bliss. It's a maintenance tool you can use to get you back on track to your **WOW** place. Once something uncomfortable happens, you simply go into a place of affirmation. You can say to yourself, *"This too shall pass, and I can do this! I'm ready. I was born for this!"* Whatever it takes for you to rebound back to that place where you were on a high, it's worth it.

This has become a way of life for me. None of this happened overnight. For example, let's say you are going to the gym, you're 165 pounds and you have some things you want to tighten up. You can't go one day a month to get those things tightened. If you want to shed 20 pounds, you have to step it up.

It requires a daily exercise of appreciation for life. It's worth it if you want to see results in your life and you want to see change. It becomes easy once you start the journey of accepting that it's going to be some work involved, and you must say, **"I'm worth it."**

The work involves me going to bed and seeing myself winning the next day. When I wake up, I visualize having the greatest day of my life. With anything negative that could happen, I apply **The Switch Mode**. This is done by thinking of those situations with a more positive outcome.

You get what you think!

It's in your mind. But just like building up your muscles in the gym, you must build the muscles in your mind. It starts one day at a time.

People want to visit church once a week and get results for a lifetime. This is a daily walk with yourself and God. This gets you in sync with God. Once you find that place, the bottom line is your alignment. You'll want to devote that time and energy to getting to know you again. It's the most amazing gift that you could ever give yourself.

Again, none of this comes fast. However, it will come as fast as you get started. Then you can experience an amazing healing that will lead you into **The Switch Mode.**

WOW Facts:

- **You can enjoy everyday life by going to bed with expectancy and getting up with expectancy**
- **This too shall pass, you can do this.**
- **You're ready, you were born for this.**
- **You're worth it.**
- **Everything negative that could happen is where you apply The Switch Mode.**

- **You get what you think about consistently.**
- **Think about GREAT and wonderful things!**

Melancholy Mood

<u>Manage Mindsets</u>

Be Free of focusing on the Negativity and the Lack. Focus on what's good in your life and the positive outcome you want.

Chapter 2

M: Manage Mindsets

The second letter in **EMBRACE** is **M** and that stands for **Manage your Mindsets**. I'm talking about being positive intentionally and being free of negativity. Intention is to do something with purpose. Focusing your intention will change and shift you to a point where you can **get unstuck.**

Being stuck is a mindset. When you wake up thinking about negative things, that negativity gains momentum. As you start your day, think of everything positive that is going to happen. That creates momentum.

It's a good idea to write down the good thoughts so you can focus on those things. What you think is what you get. Remember, if you're thinking powerful positive thoughts and you're staying focused on your goals and objectives. Those are the things that will manifest.

Be Positive Intentionally

Begin each day by asking yourself, "What's happy and joyful in my life? What's good in my life and what do I see that serves me? Observe the evidence of what's wonderful all around you.

This is a mindset that you habitually concentrate on every day. When you reprogram your negative thoughts, you realize that everybody has something good to offer if you are willing to accept it. Spend more time focusing on the good. There are many things in your life that are good and bring joy to you. At first, you may only recall a few good things. Repeat those good thoughts until they materialize.

To go from hell and heartache to bliss is a process. It is possible to go from hell and heartache to a comfortable state where the pain is over and you experience only the best of everything. Let's get into a comfortable place where you can rest easy and relax there on your way to that incredible state of **WOW**. Just ride the wave. Go with the flow.

It's all a part of the process that must be done. How do we stop accepting the negativity so that our mind is not set on a negative course? **With gratitude.** Refraining from complaining is the pivotal point. When you stop complaining and start praising, you become conscious of the fact that you've been complaining. You cannot praise and complain at the same time.

Negativity is another form of complaining. Things come up that are negative, even though sometimes, they are not of your doing. Sometimes, things just happen. Now start praising during that storm. That action will counteract anything in the negative because that's what God hears—the praise. He is your comfort in the storm.

You can't move unless God moves you. When God sees that you are shifting into what's good, into what's pleasant, then He will change the entire situation in His time. He wants to hear you. You can't get to Him by complaining and seeing negativity in front of you.

Override your negative reality with what you would like it to be. See the outcome as you would like it to be, not as it is right now. Once you see the change, then more will come. That's when the magic occurs. Your life will become what you're thinking in the positive. The more things you keep complaining about things in the negative, you keep seeing them because you're announcing them to the world.

It's only until you shift into thinking and focusing on what's good in life, what's good in you, that you start to see more of that. Can you recollect things that have been wonderful? Go back to those things even if you must borrow from the great moments of the past. This gets you where you need to be in the now versus looking at what you're lacking and highlighting it.

WOW! That is a revelation right there. Many people are comfortable in negativity, and to them it's their reality. You can get past that by filtering out the despair and focusing on the positive in your thinking.

WOW Facts:
- *Change your mind! Be positive intentionally*
- *Override your negative reality with what you would like it to be, not as it is right now.*
- *Be FREE of focusing on the negativity and lack.*
- *Focus on what's good in your life and the positive outcome you want.*

Infinite Peace

Believe Bigger

Believing bigger is the key. Believing for a WOW life takes practice.

Chapter 3:

B: Believe Bigger

When you start enjoying each day and managing your mindset, you are on the right trajectory for a blessed life. Now let's talk about the next letter **B**, which stands for *Believe Bigger.*

You deserve the best in life. God says in His Word that you deserve it if you trust Him and believe. That's what *Psalms 91* taught me. If I just take refuge in God, He starts reaching out to me. He is on His way to me. It is in Him that I put my trust.

Once you realize that you are worthy and you deserve it, the principle of **Believing Bigger** kicks in. Start easy by believing for something like, "***Somebody's going to buy*** *me lunch this week."* When that happens, most people will say, *"That's something that normally happens. But, this time they're going to buy me something specific."*

Start with something easy and watch it manifest. You'll find the power in that. Once you get in that place of belief, that thing comes to fruition. You will become a believer in the manifestation of bigger things. It doesn't matter to God if it's a sandwich or a trip to the south of France. He can make it happen if you **Believe Bigger.**

Go beyond the believing and live in the knowing. This is what I know that's coming to me. How, why, and when is not my business. *I just know.* If you live in the knowing, that's a part of the growing. The whole process of utilizing the other principles is getting you here and enjoying what you desire. Each desire will come if you stay happy long enough and believe strong enough to receive them.

We want to have the car, the husband, and the job. We think when we get them, then we're going to be happy.

But you have to get happy with or without those things. You can **Believe Big**, but you have to stay in the place of gratitude and contentment NOW. Being grateful and excited right now with what you have will bring the things that you think are bigger and better to your experience.

It's OK to **Believe Bigger** because we're worth it and we were born for it. Yet, we play small mind games thinking that we're doing God or ourselves a favor by not operating at our greatest potential.

WOW FACTS:

- *Being grateful and excited in the now with what you have will bring bigger and better to your experience.*
- *Start with something easy and watch that manifest.*
- *Once you realize that you are worthy and deserve it, the principle of Believing Bigger kicks in.*
- *Believing Bigger is the key. Believing for a WOW life takes practice.*

Duality

<u>Respond Responsibly</u>
*It is imperative to
calm yourself, seek peace, and then respond.*

Chapter 4:

R: Respond Responsibly

The **R** in **EMBRACE** stands for **Respond Responsibly**. We always have the choice to respond and not react. When we get a bit of bad news or we discover some uncomfortable secrets or a reality that we're not pleased with, our impulse is to react. Our buttons are pushed and our response is to say something ugly or do something destructive. Instead, we should take the time to take a breath and **Respond Responsibly**.

You have to make a conscious decision to respond in an intentional manner to whatever news you hear that doesn't please you, make you feel comfortable, or make you angry. You must calm yourself. You must decompress and think positively. Allow yourself to relax to a more positive state of mind.

Now is time to move into a state of calmness. Calmness is the Holy Spirit telling you to trust in God. Then you let Him order your steps. You don't order your steps. Be free of your past and that angry, depressed, vengeful person that sets you back to the old mindset. That is the place where negativity lives. You find yourself reacting rather than responding.

Once we receive negative news, it's all about relaxing, taking a deep breath, and processing. Processing allows us to get better results. The solution is the bottom line we are seeking, and to find that place with a positive mindset is the proactive way to do it. It is imperative to calm yourself, seek peace, and then respond.

When my 15-year-old daughter told me she was pregnant, all I could do was smile and say, **"God, I know you have this."** Where other family members broke down and became angry, I was able to take this information, process it, **Respond Responsibly**, and say, " *Something great is gonna come out of this."* And it did!

Give people grace. The same grace that God gives you every day for things that you do consciously or unconsciously. Most people are giving you the best that they have. When we judge others for something that they did to us, we judge them from our perspective. **Give them grace. Give them mercy. Give them some space.**

Put yourself in their position. It's not always an attack. Sometimes they're just showing you who they are. You take it personally when it's not even about you. It's about the process. **Responding Responsibly** will lead into an avenue of compassion for their situation. Take yourself out of the equation sometimes. **It's not always about you.**

Sometimes when you're talking about people who disappoint you or do things that you take personal, it could be that we are just overthinking. Once again, think the best in that situation, whatever it is, even if it was something negative. It's the other person's issue. It's their insecurity. It's their thinking and lack of self-esteem.

Everybody's different, and everybody has a different approach to love and life. It's time to have mercy, give grace, and not overthink things. If not, judgment sets in. You are worse off in judging them for what they've done to you. It may be something that's going on personally with them and has nothing at all to do with you.

The important thing in this matter is to know who you are, know whose you are, and stay in control of the positive place you're in. You earned this place therefore, it's time to own it.

WOW Facts:

Give people the same grace that God gives you every day.

Go With The Flow

All Is Well

Anticipate Awesomeness
Visualize what you desire. See it as it is and live in that place.

Chapter 5

A: Anticipate Awesomeness

That next letter is **A,** which stands for **Anticipate Awesomeness**. If you've done all the other things we've discussed, you should be able to **Anticipate Awesomeness**. When you are **Enjoying Everyday Life**, **Managing Your Mindset, Believing for Bigger** things to happen, and **Responding Responsibly,** you can **Anticipate Awesomeness**. How do you **Anticipate Awesomeness**? You expect the best and allow yourself to be blessed! **You visualize yourself already there.**

Visualization is a great part of my life. I can see my future brighter today by just staying in a place of appreciation for the now. I claim my day-to-day life to be brighter, more beautiful, and I affirm that it's delicious.

I use the visualization technique to create a spectacular future. This is a part of my habitual state of mind that helps me to **Anticipate Awesomeness.** I'm not just simply maintaining this principle—I'm living in it. I dream about it, I meditate on it, and I smile uncontrollably all the time. People want to know what's so funny and what I am smiling about all the time. It's absolutely everything. You become so giddy because God is your ally. He's high-fiving you in every moment. With that, things miraculously begin to flow for you.

Get ready because it's coming! When you **Anticipate Awesomeness,** you get the best of everything that life has to offer. If you're ready to get married, go find the dress. Visualize it. Feel what it feels like to walk down the aisle. Everything you've been waiting for can become reality if you believe. I know this to be true. I live in that belief, and take whatever steps are required to reach it. It's not my business how, why, or when, I just know it, and I anticipate it.

Embrace Your WOW Factor

Once you feel the greatness of your life and the **WOW** within you, you're unstoppable. What you anticipate will come. When one thing starts to flow, and two things start to flow, anticipate the flood because it's coming.

People who live this lifestyle **Anticipate Awesomeness**. I'm a testament to it. I live for this moment that I'm sharing with you. This is what I do day in and day out. I visualize a better life, a **WOW Life**.

This is how I allow myself to be blessed. I visualize getting something great. I invite you to join me in the anticipation of the greatness that is to come.

WOW Facts:

- *How do you Anticipate Awesomeness? By seeing and visualizing yourself already where you want to be.*
- *Once you feel the greatness of your life and the WOW within you, you're unstoppable.*
- *I live in the Power of Knowing, and whatever steps are required to reach it are not my business.*

Whatever it is, visualize it, and feel what it feels like.

Free Style

Cultivate Creativity

The mundane becomes mighty, and the mighty becomes outstanding, and the outstanding becomes absolute fulfillment.

Chapter 6

C: Cultivate Creativity

Let me share this with you since I'm talking about this **WOW** movement and mindset. How about **Cultivate Creativity**, which represents the **C** in **EMBRACE**. How do you **Cultivate Creativity**? How do you get out of that box that has boxed you in? **Just do it!** Get out of that box of self-limitation and begin to express what you see on the inside so that it manifests on the outside!

We have been brainwashed since before we started to talk by our parents and their parents. Some of them thought outside of the box and reached incredible places in life, and others by habit have taught generations to seek just enough. You must reach higher to **Cultivate** that **Creativity** on purpose. You do this the same way you were brainwashed—just reverse it. "How are you doing today?" *"I'm good. I'm all right. You know, it's OK."* These are things we say just to get by.

"I'm excellent. I'm more than enough." Shift your thinking into another mindset. Think positive. Think greatness! Be so extreme and so animated with it that it becomes your way of thinking, talking, eating, drinking, living, and your way of loving. Only greatness and pleasantries should pour out of you. That will take you to places where you've only imagined.

You see, all too many people live sheltered lives. They live a safe, "just enough lifestyle." They do simple things from day-to-day. But this day you need to say, *"I'm gonna do something different. I'm gonna try something out of the norm. I'm ready to live. I'm ready to taste the greatness of life. I'm gonna start with a new experience! I'll start by wearing this shirt with polka dots and stripes at the same time."* It's just reinventing yourself in a place and time that you've never been before. It's a newness that's fresh and wonderful.

The mundane becomes mighty and outstanding. Ultimately you reach a state of pure fulfillment. You get so full that you become contagious. That's what we want. We want to be so full that we're contagious and people want to know, *"How did you get to this place where you're so free? I've never seen you this way before. I want some of that!"*

The formula for **Cultivating** that **Creativity** is already within you. Just operate within that **WOW**. In that process, if you do all the following things, it puts you in a place where you:

- **Enjoy Everyday Life**
- **Manage Your Mindset**
- **Believe Bigger**
- **Respond Responsibly**
- **Anticipate the Awesomeness**
- **Cultivate Creativity**

Think outside of the box. Now prepare yourself for the greatness that's awaiting you.

WOW Facts:

- *The mundane becomes mighty, the mighty becomes outstanding, and the outstanding becomes pure fulfillment.*
- *Too many people live sheltered lives. They live a safe, "just enough" lifestyle.*
- *The formula for Cultivating Creativity is already within you. Just operate within the WOW!*

Epiphany

__Paradox__

<u>Expect EXTRA</u>

If you relax and focus on knowing what you do want, you can have more.

Chapter 7

E: Expect Extra

This leads us to the final **E** in **EMBRACE**, and how to, *Expect Extra Every Day.* Be free of limiting yourself. Let God bless you with overflow. Believe more is possible! Know that you can have a great job, a wonderful relationship, and do anything that you desire. It's OK to expect the overflow.

Throughout the Word, God shows us that we can have the things we desire. **It's us putting limitations on God.** It's our lack of faith. Having a lack of faith and disbelief keeps you stagnant and paralyzed in fear.

Once you get a taste of what **your faith and your knowing** can bring to you, then you begin to do it naturally. These principles become a way of life. In Matthew 7:7 it reads, "**Ask and it shall be given**..." God made it easy, and we made it hard.

We make it difficult. It's been here all the time. This is our gift and our birthright. We have gotten so used to being not enough, that we limit ourselves. Every area that we're coming up empty in is a result of our own limited thinking. We're weighed down with the day-to-day life issues.

If you could just relax and focus on knowing what you want, you can have more of it. You must say what you want. You must speak your desires out loud and write them down. Then imagine what that would feel like if it were already manifested.

All the things that I've been sharing throughout this whole book will become evident. It allows you to become an integral part of the process. These things are yours for the asking, but you've got to ask for them. If you're not ready, then it won't come.

If you're not exercising your mind to believe you can have what you truly desire, then you're going to come up empty. You must apply these principles to have everything you could ever imagine. Once you get in the **WOW** rhythm it takes you over.

Life is a beautiful dance that's non-stop. If you get out of rhythm, simply get back in step. It's OK to be a little offbeat. Just make a maintenance call to the Most High God. Then you start over again, and the rhythm keeps going, and you are now developing into a beautiful dance.

Recap these seven principles of *Embracing Your WOW*:
- **Enjoy Everyday Life**
- **Manage Mindsets**
- **Believe Bigger**
- **Respond Responsibly**
- **Anticipate Awesomeness**
- **Cultivate Creativity**
- **Expect Extra**

Embrace Your WOW Factor

To initiate these principles, I've created a journal that allows you to apply, reflect, and grow. This is a powerful and rewarding experience.

After Thoughts

The transformation was painful and not very glamorous. I fought it each step of the way. The more I complained, the worse it got. As I relaxed, I moved into the silence . This gave me a sense of peace. I took refuge in the solitude. That's when I connected the dots and realized the power from within. I was even more eager to be still and be quiet. I called it, " My developmental stage."

"All of that to get to this," I asked? Yes, it was mandatory! It was the gateway to God.

I had several opportunities to go freely, but I chose bondage as opposed to freedom. Now that I am here, I am free of resisting. I embrace the process, yet foresee obstacles as my pathway to a lesson.

Instead of asking, "Why?" I simply asked, "What? What's next?" I wonder what it is that God will teach me about me that will aid others. I graciously accept the honor of being used for the glory of God.

Freedom comes with a cost. Free insinuates no payment, yet we still pay the price of having to explain or defend ourselves for that beautiful thing called Freedom. If you're like me, secure in your right to be whoever you are, then be Free of Apologies and Free of Excuses. Now, carry on in The Divine Light. Let others see your brightness as they step out of their box to join the freedom.

I took delight in material things because I thought they would bring me happiness. It worked for a minute as I accumulated a bunch of tangible things. When I started to partner with God, and He soothed my spirit, this is when He was able to bless me with unspeakable joy.

When you live in the WOW, you live in the now. The past is irrelevant. What's coming isn't as important as this moment. Live in the moment. Become everything that God created you to be in that place you reside. This is where the magic happens!

The best will manifest if you focus on what is good, what is just, and what is God, leaving all the contrasting thoughts to Him who can fix all things. You can relax now in the your WOW.

What did I gain from this experience? The book! This book was a journey that led me back to my true self, The WOW WOMAN OF GOD that I lost. She has now found her way home. The wondering soul has found the source of all that is WOW.

Declaration of WOW

- Today, I declare and affirm my **WOW Factor.**
- Today, I embrace the fact that I can and will operate within all of the power of my **WOW Factor.**
- I express for the world to know that I am **Worthy of Winning.**
- I accept my own self-worth.
- I am deserving of living and fulfilling my dreams, goals, and aspirations.
- I am living out my legacy as a person of worth.

- I embrace every aspect of my **WOW Factor.**
- I am awesomely created and have been designed for greatness and an incredible destiny.
- I will **Enjoy Everyday Life, Manage my Mindset, Believe Bigger, Respond Responsibly, Anticipate Awesomeness, Cultivate Creativity** and **Expect Extra Every Day.**
- Today I EMBRACE my **WOW Factor.**
- Today, I am Free of Apologies and Free of Excuses.

Signature: _____

Date: _____

EMBRACE Your WOW Journal

Use this journal to write down your thoughts, plans, and moments of WOW.

Mirror Image

Day 1: Enjoy Everyday Life

Spend time with God and yourself. In the morning, during the course of the day, and in times of trouble, don't forget to apply your SWITCH mode.

_____

_____

_____

_____

_____

_____

_____

_____

_____

_____

_____

_____

_____

_____

Embrace Your WOW Factor

_____

_____

_____

_____

_____

_____

_____

_____

_____

_____

_____

_____

_____

_____

_____

_____

_____

_____

_____

_____

_____

Embrace Your WOW Factor

_____

_____

_____

_____

_____

_____

_____

_____

_____

_____

_____

_____

_____

_____

_____

_____

_____

_____

_____

Embrace Your WOW Factor

_____

_____

_____

_____

_____

_____

_____

_____

_____

_____

_____

_____

_____

_____

_____

_____

_____

_____

_____

_____

_____

_____

Day 2: Manage Mindset

Be free of focusing on the negativity and lack. Focus on what's good in your life and the positive outcome you want.

Embrace Your WOW Factor

_____

_____

_____

_____

_____

_____

_____

_____

_____

_____

_____

_____

_____

_____

_____

_____

_____

_____

_____

_____

Embrace Your WOW Factor

_____

_____

_____

_____

_____

_____

_____

_____

_____

_____

_____

_____

_____

_____

_____

_____

_____

_____

_____

_____

Embrace Your WOW Factor

_____

_____

_____

_____

_____

_____

_____

_____

_____

_____

_____

_____

_____

_____

_____

_____

_____

_____

_____

_____

_____

Day 3: Believe Bigger

Believing Bigger is the key. Believing for a WOW Life takes practice.

_____

_____

_____

_____

_____

_____

_____

_____

_____

_____

_____

_____

_____

_____

_____

_____

_____

_____

Embrace Your WOW Factor

_____

_____

_____

_____

_____

_____

_____

_____

_____

_____

_____

_____

_____

_____

_____

_____

_____

_____

_____

_____

Embrace Your WOW Factor

_____

_____

_____

_____

_____

_____

_____

_____

_____

_____

_____

_____

_____

_____

_____

_____

_____

_____

_____

_____

_____

Embrace Your WOW Factor

_____

_____

_____

_____

_____

_____

_____

_____

_____

_____

_____

_____

_____

_____

_____

_____

_____

_____

_____

_____

_____

Day 4: Respond Responsibly

Be calm, collected, and conscious of the moment.

_____

_____

_____

_____

_____

_____

_____

_____

_____

_____

_____

_____

_____

_____

_____

_____

_____

_____

_____

_____

Embrace Your WOW Factor

_____

_____

_____

_____

_____

_____

_____

_____

_____

_____

_____

_____

_____

_____

_____

_____

_____

_____

_____

_____

Day 5: Anticipate Awesomeness

Visualize what you desire. See it as if it is and live in that place.

_____

_____

_____

_____

_____

_____

_____

_____

_____

_____

_____

_____

_____

_____

_____

_____

_____

Embrace Your WOW Factor

_____

_____

_____

_____

_____

_____

_____

_____

_____

_____

_____

_____

_____

_____

_____

_____

_____

_____

_____

_____

_____

Embrace Your WOW Factor

_____

_____

_____

_____

_____

_____

_____

_____

_____

_____

_____

_____

_____

_____

_____

_____

_____

_____

_____

_____

_____

_____

_____

Embrace Your WOW Factor

_____

_____

_____

_____

_____

_____

_____

_____

_____

_____

_____

_____

_____

_____

_____

_____

_____

_____

_____

_____

Day 6: Cultivate Creativity

The mundane becomes mighty, the mighty becomes outstanding, and the outstanding becomes absolute fulfillment.

_____

_____

_____

_____

_____

_____

_____

_____

_____

_____

_____

_____

_____

_____

_____

_____

_____

Embrace Your WOW Factor

_____

_____

_____

_____

_____

_____

_____

_____

_____

_____

_____

_____

_____

_____

_____

_____

_____

_____

_____

_____

Embrace Your WOW Factor

_____

_____

_____

_____

_____

_____

_____

_____

_____

_____

_____

_____

_____

_____

_____

_____

_____

_____

_____

_____

Embrace Your WOW Factor

_____

_____

_____

_____

_____

_____

_____

_____

_____

_____

_____

_____

_____

_____

_____

_____

_____

_____

_____

Day 7: Expect Extra

If you relax and focus on knowing what you want, you can have more of it.

_____

_____

_____

_____

_____

_____

_____

_____

_____

_____

_____

_____

_____

_____

_____

_____

Embrace Your WOW Factor

_____

_____

_____

_____

_____

_____

_____

_____

_____

_____

_____

_____

_____

_____

_____

_____

_____

_____

_____

_____

_____

Embrace Your WOW Factor

Embrace Your WOW Factor

_____

_____

_____

_____

_____

_____

_____

_____

_____

_____

_____

_____

_____

_____

_____

_____

_____

_____

_____

_____

_____

About the Author

Who is Paris Love?
She is a multifaceted, multitalented, Life Stylist whose goal is to impact others by inspiring them to love themselves from the inside out.

As the co-owner of Hair Lounge Dallas Salon & Art Gallery, she's inspired women's new growth, not just hair: but through the arts, via self-awareness, and lifestyle transformations.

As a visual artist, Paris' original pieces have Wowed art lovers, and have been featured nationwide.

Paris' image consulting business, **Be The Wow Factor,** which inspired this book, addresses how to embrace your spirit as you transform your style. Her objective is to aid in bringing out the authentic you that has laid dormant waiting to be freed.

As an author of her first book, **Embrace Your WOW FACTOR; 7 Ways To Love Yourself, Free Of Apologies And Free Of Excuses,** Paris Love reveals how she found her way, first by reaching up, then reaching deep inside of herself to find her, **WOW Factor.** She says every woman has one. She's on a mission to help you celebrate yours! Paris wrote the book on how to set you free!

MISSION STATEMENT

Teaching women to love themselves from within, free of apologies and free of excuses!